BENJAMIN FRANKLIN BIOGR/

By David Right

CW00471581

ALL COPYRIGHTS RESERVED 2017
All Rights Reserved

Copyright 2017 by David Right - All rights reserved.

This document is geared towards providing exact and reliable information in regards to the topic and issue covered. The publication is sold with the idea that the publisher is not required to render accounting, officially permitted, or otherwise, qualified services. If advice is necessary, legal or professional, a practiced individual in the profession should be ordered.

- From a Declaration of Principles which was accepted and approved equally by a Committee of the American Bar Association and a Committee of Publishers and Associations.

In no way is it legal to reproduce, duplicate, or transmit any part of this document in either electronic means or in printed format. Recording of this publication is strictly prohibited and any storage of this document is not allowed unless with written permission from the publisher. All rights reserved.

The information provided herein is stated to be truthful and consistent, in that any liability, in terms of inattention or otherwise, by any usage or abuse of any policies, processes, or directions contained within is the solitary and utter responsibility of the recipient reader. Under no circumstances will any legal responsibility or blame be held against the publisher for any reparation, damages, or monetary loss due to the information herein, either directly or indirectly.

Respective authors own all copyrights not held by the publisher.

The information herein is offered for informational purposes solely, and is universal as so. The presentation of the information is without contract or any type of guarantee assurance.

PREFACE

Benjamin Franklin was born in Boston on January 17, 1706. He was the tenth son of soap maker, Josiah Franklin. Benjamin's mother was Abiah Folger, the second wife of Josiah. In all, Josiah would father 17 children.

Josiah intended for Benjamin to enter into the clergy. However, Josiah could only afford to send his son to school for one year and clergymen needed years of schooling. But, as young Benjamin loved to read he had him apprenticed to his brother James, who was a printer. After helping James compose pamphlets and set type which was grueling work, 12-year-old Benjamin would sell their products in the streets. Read on.

Table of Contents

Benjamin Franklin is best known as one of the Founding Fathers who drafted the Declaration of Independence and the Constitution of the United States.

IN THESE GROUPS

QUOTES

"We are all born ignorant, but one must work hard to remain stupid."

—Benjamin Franklin

Synopsis

Born in Boston in 1706, Benjamin Franklin helped to draft the Declaration of Independence and the U.S. Constitution, and he negotiated the 1783 Treaty of Paris, which ended the Revolutionary War. His scientific pursuits included investigations into electricity, mathematics, and mapmaking. A printer and writer known for his wit and wisdom, Franklin was a polymath who published Poor Richard's Almanack, invented bifocal glasses and organized the first successful American lending library.

Early Life

Benjamin Franklin was born on January 17, 1706, in Boston in what was then known as the Massachusetts Bay Colony. His father, English-born soap and candle maker Josiah Franklin, had seven children with first wife, Anne Child, and 10 more with second wife, Abiah Folger. Ben was his 15th child and youngest son.

Ben learned to read at an early age, and despite his success at the Boston Latin School, he stopped his formal schooling at 10 to work full-time in his cash-strapped father's candle and soap shop. Dipping wax and cutting wicks didn't fire the young boy's imagination, however. Perhaps to dissuade him from going to sea as one of his brothers had done, Josiah apprenticed Ben at 12 to his brother James at his print shop.

Although James mistreated and frequently beat his younger brother, Ben learned a great deal about newspaper publishing and adopted a similar brand of subversive politics under the printer's tutelage. When James refused to publish any of his brother's writing, 16-year-old Ben adopted the pseudonym Mrs. Silence Dogood, and "her" 14 imaginative and witty letters delighted readers of his brother's newspaper, The New England Courant. James grew angry, however, when he learned that his apprentice had penned the letters. Tired of his brother's "harsh and tyrannical" behavior, Ben fled Boston in 1723 although he had three years remaining on a legally binding contract with his master. He escaped to New York before settling in Philadelphia, which became his home base for the rest of his life.

Franklin found work with another printer in Philadelphia and lodged at the home of John Read, where he met and courted his landlord's daughter Deborah. Encouraged by Pennsylvania Governor William Keith to set up his own print shop, Franklin left for London in 1724 to purchase supplies from stationers, booksellers and printers. When the teenager arrived in England, however, he felt duped when Keith's letters of introduction never arrived as promised. Although forced to find work at London's print shops, Franklin took full advantage of the city's pleasures—attending theater performances, mingling with the populace in coffee houses and continuing his lifelong passion for reading. A self-taught swimmer who crafted his own wooden flippers, Franklin performed long-distance swims on the Thames River. (In 1968, he was inducted as an honorary member of the International Swimming Hall of Fame.)

In 1725 Franklin published his first pamphlet, "A Dissertation upon Liberty and Necessity, Pleasure and Pain," which argued that humans lack free will and, thus, are not morally responsible for their actions. (Franklin later repudiated this thought and burned all but one copy of the pamphlet still in his possession.)

Franklin returned to Philadelphia in 1726 to find that Deborah Read had married in the interim, only to be abandoned by her husband just months after the wedding. In the next few years he held varied jobs such as bookkeeper, shopkeeper and currency cutter. He returned to a familiar trade in 1728 when he printed paper currency in New Jersey before partnering with a friend to open his own print shop in Philadelphia that published government pamphlets and books. In 1730 Franklin was named the official printer of Pennsylvania. By that time, he had formed the "Junto," a social and self-improvement study group for young men that met every Friday to debate morality, philosophy and politics. When Junto members sought to expand their reading choices, Franklin helped to incorporate America's first subscription library, the Library Company of Philadelphia, in 1731.

Prominent Citizen

In 1729 Franklin published another pamphlet, "A Modest En□uiry into The Nature and Necessity of a Paper Currency," which advocated for an increase in the money supply to stimulate the economy. With the cash Franklin earned from his money-related treatise, he was able to purchase The Pennsylvania Gazette newspaper from a former boss. Under his ownership, the struggling newspaper was transformed into the most widely read paper in the colonies and became one of the first to turn a profit. He had less luck in 1732 when he launched the first German-language newspaper in the colonies, the short-lived Philadelphische Zeitung.

After the future Founding Father rekindled his romance with Deborah Read, he took her as his common-law wife in 1730. Around that time, Franklin fathered a son, William, out of wedlock who was taken in by the couple. The pair's first son, Francis, was born in 1732, but he died four years later of smallpox. The couple's only daughter, Sarah, was born in 1743.

Franklin's prominence and success grew during the 1730s, especially with the publication of Poor Richard's Almanack at the end of 1732. In addition to weather forecasts, astronomical information and poetry, the almanac—which Franklin published for 25 consecutive years—included proverbs and Franklin's witty maxims such as "Early to bed and early to rise, makes a man healthy, wealthy and wise" and "He that lies down with dogs, shall rise up with fleas."

Franklin amassed real estate and businesses and organized the volunteer Union Fire Company to counteract dangerous fire hazards in Philadelphia. He joined the Freemasons in 1731 and was eventually elected grand master of the Masons of Pennsylvania.

The 1740s saw Franklin expanding into entrepreneurship with invention of the Franklin stove, which provided more heat with less fuel, and also into scientific pursuits. His 1743 pamphlet "A Proposal for Promoting Useful Knowledge" underscored his interests and served as the founding document of the American Philosophical Society, the first scientific society in the colonies.

By 1748, the 42-year-old Franklin had become one of the richest men in Pennsylvania. He turned his printing business over to a partner to give him more time to conduct scientific experiments. He moved into a new house in 1748 and acquired the first of his slaves to work in the new home and in the print shop. Franklin's views on slavery evolved over the following decades to the point that he considered the institution inherently evil, and thus, he freed his slaves in the 1760s.

He became a soldier in the Pennsylvania militia at the age of 42, but his abiding interest in electricity was ignited at this time, too. His investigations into electrical phenomena were complied into "Experiments and Observations on Electricity," published in England in 1751. He conducted the famous kite-and-key experiment in 1752 to demonstrate that lighting was electricity. He invented the lightning rod and coined new electricity-related terms that are still part of the lexicon, such as battery, charge, conductor and electrify.

A prolific inventor, Franklin developed bifocals that could be used for both distance and reading. He is credited with inventing the first rocking chair, flexible catheter, and American penny. He even devised a new "scheme" for the alphabet that proposed to eliminate the letters C, J, Q, W, X and Y as redundant.

Franklin's inventions took on a musical bent as well. In 1761 he commenced development of the armonica, a musical instrument composed of spinning glass bowls on a shaft. Both Ludwig van Beethoven and Wolfgang Amadeus Mozart composed music for the strange instrument.

His self-education earned him honorary degrees from Harvard, Yale, England's Oxford University and Scotland's University of St. Andrews in Scotland. In 1749, Franklin wrote a pamphlet relating to the education of youth in Pennsylvania that resulted in the establishment of the Academy of Philadelphia, now the University of Pennsylvania.

Public Service

Franklin became a member of Philadelphia's city council in 1748 and a justice of the peace the following year. In 1751 Franklin was elected a Philadelphia alderman and a representative to the Pennsylvania Assembly, a position to which he was re-elected annually until 1764. Two years later, he accepted a royal appointment as deputy postmaster general of North America.

When the French and Indian War began in 1754, Franklin called on the colonies to band together for their common defense, which he dramatized in The Pennsylvania Gazette with a cartoon of a snake cut into sections with the caption "Join or Die." He represented Pennsylvania at the Albany Congress, which adopted his proposal to create a unified government for the 13 colonies. Franklin's "Plan of Union," however, failed to be ratified by the colonies.

In 1757 he was appointed by the Pennsylvania Assembly to serve as the colony's agent in England. Franklin sailed to London to negotiate a long-standing dispute with the proprietors of the colony, the Penn family, taking William and his two slaves but leaving behind Deborah and Sarah. He spent most of the next two decades in London, where he was drawn to the high society and intellectual salons of the cosmopolitan city.

After Franklin returned to Philadelphia in 1762, he toured the colonies to inspect its post offices and William took office as New Jersey's royal governor, a position his father arranged through his political connections in the British government. After Franklin lost his seat in the Pennsylvania Assembly in 1764, he returned to London as the colony's agent without Deborah, who refused to leave Philadelphia. It would be the last time the couple saw each other. Franklin would not return home before Deborah passed away in 1774 from a stroke at the age of 66.

He returned to London at a tense time in the relations between Great Britain and the American colonies. Parliament's passage of the Stamp Act in March 1765 imposed a highly unpopular tax on all printed materials for commercial and legal use in the colonies. Since Franklin purchased stamps for his printing business and nominated a friend as the Pennsylvania stamp distributor, some colonists thought Franklin implicitly supported the new tax, and rioters in Philadelphia even threatened his house. Franklin's passionate denunciation of the tax in testimony before Parliament, however, contributed to the Stamp Act's repeal in 1766.

Two years later he penned a pamphlet, "Causes of the American Discontents before 1768," and he soon became an agent for Massachusetts, Georgia and New Jersey as well. Franklin fanned the flames of revolution by sending the inflammatory private letters of Massachusetts Governor Thomas Hutchinson, which called for the restriction of the rights of colonists, to America where they caused a firestorm after their publication by Boston newspapers. In the wake of the scandal, Franklin was removed as deputy postmaster general, and he returned to North America in 1775 as a devotee of the patriot cause.

Always intellectually curious, Franklin began to speculate on his return trip across the Atlantic Ocean about why the westbound trip always took longer, and his measurements of ocean temperatures led to his discovery of the existence of the Gulf Stream, the knowledge of which served to cut two weeks off the previous sailing time from Europe to North America.

In 1775, Franklin was elected to the Second Continental Congress and appointed the first postmaster general for the colonies. And in 1776, he was appointed commissioner to Canada and was one of five men to draft the Declaration of Independence. Franklin's support for the patriot cause put him at odds with his Loyalist son. When the New Jersey militia stripped William Franklin of his post as royal governor and imprisoned him, his father chose not to intercede on his behalf. After voting for independence, Franklin was elected commissioner to France and set sail to negotiate a treaty for the country's military and financial support.

Later Years

Much has been made of Franklin's years in Paris, chiefly his romantic life, as essentially the first U.S. ambassador to France. After Deborah's death, Franklin had a rich romantic life in his nine years abroad. At the age of 74, he even proposed marriage to a widow named Madame Helvetius, but she rejected him.

Franklin was embraced in France as much, if not more, for his wit and intellectual standing in the scientific community as for his status as a political appointee from a fledging country. His reputation facilitated respect and entrees into closed communities, including that of King Louis XVI. And it was his adept diplomacy that led to the Treaty of Paris in 1783, which ended the Revolutionary War.

After almost a decade in France, Franklin returned to the United States in 1785. He was elected in 1787 to represent Pennsylvania at the Constitutional Convention, which drafted and ratified the new U.S. Constitution. The oldest delegate at the age of 81, Franklin initially supported proportional representation in Congress, but he fashioned the Great Compromise that resulted in proportional representation in the House of Representatives and equal representation by state in the Senate.

Franklin helped found the Society for Political Inquiries, dedicated to improving knowledge of government, in 1787. He also became more vociferous in his opposition to slavery. He served as president of the Pennsylvania Society for Promoting the Abolition of Slavery, wrote many tracts urging the abolition of slavery and petitioned the U.S. Congress in 1790 to end slavery and the slave trade.

Death and Legacy

Benjamin Franklin died on April 17, 1790, in Philadelphia, Pennsylvania, at the home of his daughter, Sarah Bache. He was 84, suffered from gout and had complained of ailments for some time, completing the final codicil to his will a little more than a year and a half prior to his death. He bequeathed most of his estate to Sarah and very little to William, whose opposition to the patriot cause still stung him. He also donated money that funded scholarships, schools and museums in Boston and Philadelphia.

Franklin had actually written his epitaph when he was 22: "The body of B. Franklin, Printer (Like the Cover of an Old Book Its Contents torn Out And Stript of It's Lettering and Gilding) Lies Here, Food for Worms. But the Work shall not be Lost; For it will (as he Believ'd) Appear once More In a New and More Elegant Edition Revised and Corrected By the Author." In the end, however, the stone on the grave he shared with his wife in the cemetery of Philadelphia's Christ Church reads simply, "Benjamin and Deborah Franklin 1790."

The image of Benjamin Franklin that has come down through history, along with the likeness on the $100 bill, is something of a caricature—a bald man in a frock coat holding a kite string with a key attached. But the scope of things he applied himself to was so broad it seems a shame. Founding universities and libraries, the post office, shaping the foreign policy of the fledgling United States, drafting the Declaration of Independence, publishing newspapers, warming us with the Franklin stove, pioneering advances in science, letting us see with bifocals and lighting our way with electricity—all from a man who never finished school but shaped his life through abundant reading and experience, a strong moral compass and an unflagging commitment to civic duty. Franklin illumined corners of American life that still have the lingering glow of his attention. He was a true polymath and entrepreneur, which is no doubt why he is often called the "First American."

Born in Boston in 1706, Benjamin Franklin was the youngest son of Josiah Franklin and Abiah Folger. It was Josiah's second family and Benjamin was his tenth son; there would be no great inheritance for Benjamin, everything would have to be earned on his own. For young Ben Franklin, childhood included only a few years of formal education which only sparked his curiosity and set him on a path of intense independent study. At the age of 12, he was apprenticed to his brother James who was a printer and for Ben Franklin, early life got difficult. He excelled at work in the print shop and after his brother founded a newspaper called The New England Courant, young Benjamin got the idea that he wanted to write and share his opinions. James would have none of it, but Benjamin was a clever boy; he wrote lengthy, opinionated letters under the pseudonym Mrs. Silence Dogood and sent them into the paper anonymously. Although these letters garnered alot of attention for the newspaper, they also brought controversy and James was very upset when Benjamin admitted that he was indeed the author. It was around this time that Benjamin Franklin ran away to Philadelphia and began an independent career in a new print shop.

Benjamin Franklin's childhood also included his first invention. As a lover of the open water and a strong swimmer, Franklin wanted to go faster. Imitating nature, he devised and constructed wooden paddles that became false flippers worn on both his hands and feet. This simple and sensible invention helped him maximize the potential force of each stroke and propelled him to speeds that would be difficult or impossible for the strongest of unaided swimmers. This experience shows that Benjamin Franklin, as a child, was already tackling life's little problems with sensibility and innovation.

In Philadelphia, Franklin quickly became noticed for his talents and was recruited by the Governor of Pennsylvania for a mission to buy printing equipment in London. Although Franklin arrived in London in 1724 at the age of 18, the Governor's letters of credit never showed up and Benjamin was stranded in England for two years. It was only a loan from a wealthy Philadelphia merchant that allowed Franklin to return and for the next year he had to work off the debt. Benjamin Franklin, as a kid, had shown sparks of genius, and as a young adult, his ambition carried him to greater heights. In 1727, Franklin helped to establish a society of young, like-minded men of enlightened philosophy and great ambition who called themselves the Junto. Only a year later, Franklin and his business partner founded The Pennsylvania Gazette out of their mutually owned print shop. For Benjamin Franklin, early life was looking up. In 1731, Franklin wrote the charter for the world's first subscription library which he opened with the help of his Junto brethren and called the Library Company. This organization still exists today and now houses thousands of important documents from U.S. and World History.

FRANKLIN SCHOOLING

Surprisingly, although Benjamin Franklin was an accomplished inventor, scientist, writer, philosopher, statesmen, diplomat, and abolitionist, he did not actually graduate from the finest institutions of higher learning. Benjamin Franklin's greatest education came not from any type of formal school but instead from his own life and experience.

Here's what is known about Franklin's formal education:

Franklin's father sent Benjamin to the Boston Latin School at age eight. This public school designed to provide education in the humanities to all boys regardless of their social class. This was common practice at the time, especially for those who would eventually enter into ministry. Franklin's father aspired that Benjamin would one day be a preacher, and thus sent him along this traditional track of education.

Benjamin's father started to have second thoughts about Benjamin's potential future in the ministry and decided, instead, to transfer Benjamin to a school that focused on subjects like writing and mathematics which would be practical if Benjamin was to enter the family business.

Benjamin was sent to the George Brownell's English school for writing and arithmetic less than a year after he began at the Boston Latin School. Franklin immediately excelled, most of all in the field of writing.

Franklin stayed at George Brownell's school until he was 10, when family finances caused the need for Benjamin to stop his formal education in order to take up a post at his father's candle-making store.

At age 12, Benjamin took an interest in the business of printing, especially given his voracious appetite for reading and writing. As a result, Ben assumed an apprenticeship in the printing office of his brother James, where he learned much about the process of printing.

Further education came directly from Franklin's personal studies and communications with others. There is no additional evidence of formal schooling.

By reviewing his history, it can be said that where Benjamin Franklin went to school is not as important as his contribution to history and the knowledge he brought to bare as a founding father of our country.

WHY WAS HE SO IMPORTANT IN THE UNITED STATES

Benjamin Franklin founded or helped found numerous organizations and institutions—fire-fighting clubs, academies, hospitals, libraries, and insurance companies. Although important, his roles in those institutions take a back seat to his part in helping found the United States of America.

Of all the founding fathers, Franklin has the unique distinction of having signed all three of the major documents that freed the colonies from British rule and established the United States as an independent nation: the Declaration of Independence, The Treaty of Paris, and the United States Constitution.

Declaration of Independence

In 1776, Franklin was appointed by the Continental Congress to a committee charged with drafting a formal document to justify the colonies' decision of severing political ties with Britain. The other members of the committee included Thomas Jefferson, John Adams, Robert Livingston and Roger Sherman. The committee gave Jefferson the task of writing the first draft. Franklin, although a talented writer, took a back seat in drafting the document, blaming his lack of participation on poor health.

Jefferson sent his finished draft to Franklin for review. Franklin put on his editor's hat, but made only a few slight changes to Jefferson's prose. When the draft was submitted to Congress, however, sentence after sentence was either deleted or changed, much to the dismay of Jefferson.

Later, Jefferson recalled a story that Franklin told him as members of Congress picked away at the draft.

"I have made a rule, whenever in my power, to avoid becoming the draughtsman of papers to be reviewed by a public body. I took my lesson from an incident which I will relate to you. When I was a journeyman printer, one of my companions, a apprentice hatter, having served out his time, was about to open shop for himself. His first concern was to have a handsome signboard, with a proper inscription. He composed it in these words, 'John Thompson, Hatter, makes and sells hats for ready money,' with a figure of an hat subjoined. But thought he would submit it to his friends for their amendments. The first he showed it to thought the word 'Hatter' tautologous, because followed by the words 'makes hats,' which showed he was a hatter. It was struck out. The next observed that the word 'makes' might as well be omitted, because his customers would not care who made the hats. If good and to their mind, they would buy them, by whomsoever made. He struck it out. A third said he thought the words 'for ready money' were useless, as it was not the custom of the place to sell on credit. Every one who purchased expected to pay. They were parted with, and the inscription now stood, 'John Thompson sells hats.' 'Sells hats!' says the next friend. 'Why, nobody will expect you to give them away. What then is the use of that word?' It was stricken out, and 'hats' followed it, the rather as there was one painted on the board. So the inscription was reduced ultimately to 'John Thompson,' with the figure of a hat subjoined."

After several drafts, Congress approved the Declaration of Independence on July 4, 1776. The actual document was not signed until August when Benjamin Franklin signed his name along with the fifty-five other representatives of the thirteen colonies.

The Treaty of Paris

In 1781, Benjamin Franklin was in France. He had been in Paris since 1776, as Minister to France. He had successfully negotiated a treaty of alliance between the French and the united colonies and had secured loans from the French government which helped finance the American revolution against the British.

Franklin understood the French and knew that real diplomacy wasn't accomplished at the negotiating table, but at the dinner table. He spent a great deal of time in the salons and at dinner parties where things could be discussed in an informal manner. In this way, he won the trust and respect of the French court.

In the meantime, John Adams felt that Franklin was just enjoying himself while he and John Jay worked.

Although the Continental Congress wanted to negotiate a treaty directly with Great Britain, the French wanted to arrange for a three-way treaty that would end the war between France and England, as well as between England and the colonies. There was some concern on the part of the Congress, as well as other commission members, that Franklin might be unduly influenced by France in the negotiations. Months passed and various offers and counteroffers were made by the former colonies and Great Britain. In addition, France was negotiating settlements with Great Britain that involved portions of the North American continent.

Adams and Jay made an end run around France to negotiate a treaty directly with Great Britain. The British made an incredible offer, one that gave the Americans almost more than they were demanding. Franklin recognized that the British offer was the best that could be had. The French were offended that the Americans had gone behind their back. Franklin used his connections and his diplomatic skills to convince the French that Adams and Jay had acted out of lack of propriety, not hostility. In late November 1782, the Paris pact was signed and sent back to Great Britain and the American Congress for ratification. Thanks to Franklin's diplomacy, along with Adams' and Jay's work, the United States was recognized as a separate and e ual nation by the world's great superpowers, France, and Great Britain.

The Constitution

Although Franklin was eighty-one years old and in generally poor health, he participated as a delegate to the Constitutional Convention in Philadelphia with George Washington presiding. Many of the delegates had widely different ideas about how the country should be organized and run, including Franklin. For instance, he believed that executive power was too great to be placed in the hands of one person and that a committee was a much better option. Alexander Hamilton, on the other end of the argument, wanted a single executive, appointed for life. The convention chose a single executive with a limited term.

For the legislative branch, Franklin favored a unicameral legislature. His beliefs were not favored by the majority, however. The convention deliberated over a way to provide equal representation for both small and large states. Franklin helped break the deadlock and pave the way for what became known as the "great compromise." Larger states would have their way in the lower house of the legislature, where representatives would be selected according to the population. The upper house or Senate would have an equal number of senators from each state.

In September 1787, the Constitution was completed, but many delegates were disgruntled. Franklin wrote an impassioned speech, in which he used his persuasive powers to urge all delegates to sign the Constitution. Franklin admitted that it was an imperfect document but probably the best they could expect. Following the speech, the Constitution was signed. To Franklin's disappointment, some delegates still refused to sign.

As the representatives signed the Constitution, Franklin watched. The president's chair was at the front of the hall, and a sun was painted on the back of the chair. Franklin told some of the members near him that it was always difficult for painters to show the difference between the rising sun and the setting sun. He said that during the convention he had often looked at the painted sun and wondered "...whether it was rising or setting. But now at length I have the happiness to know that it is a rising and not a setting sun."

A bachelor in his twenties was frowned upon and Franklin at age 24 was set to find a wife.

Deborah Read, who he had courted before going to England, had married Roger Potter during his absence. In 1727 Potter had ran away to the West Indies escaping creditors.

The wife of Thomas Godfrey, a mathematician who lived in part of Franklin's house with his family and Junto member, tried to make a match between Franklin and a relative's daughter. Franklin started courting the girl and expected a large dowry for their marriage. He had planned to use the dowry to pay the remaining debt for the printing house which added to 100 pounds. The parents declined to pay and the relationship was terminated as well as his friendship with Thomas Godfrey.

Small Pox inoculation - Franklin's son

Method and Success of Inoculating the Small-Pox in New England, 1722. Houghton Library—Harvard College Library

On September 1 1730, Benjamin Franklin married Deborah Read. They entered a common-law agreement which protected them from bigamy if her runaway husband returned.

Deborah assisted in the business by folding and stitching pamphlets, tending shop, purchasing old linen rags for paper makers. He found her a "good and faithful helpmate".

Around the time they married Franklin took custody of an illegitimate child, William. The name of the mother remains a mystery.

The couple had two children. The first was Francis Folger Franklin born October 1732. The second, Sarah Franklin born in 1743. In 1736 Francis, who was 4 years old, died from small pox. He had not been inoculated. Inoculation had proven successful after the 1721 outbreak in Boston when 5,889 Bostonians had smallpox, and 844 died of it. About Francis's death Franklin wrote in his autobiography:

"In 1736 I lost one of my sons, a fine boy of four years old, by the smallpox taken in the common way. I long regretted bitterly and still regret that I had not given it to him by inoculation. This I mention for the sake of the parents who omit that operation, on the supposition that they should never forgive themselves if a child died under it; my example showing that the regret may be the same either way, and that, therefore, the safer should be chosen."

In his day, Benjamin Franklin was Steve Jobs, Thomas Edison, Mark Zuckerberg, and Henry Ford, all rolled into one. Here's a look at his most enduring innovations and inventions on January 17, Ben's birthday.

Like the above-mentioned people, Franklin invented his own widely used devices, or found innovative ways to improve on other people's inventions.

His reputation as a scientist, inventor, author, and statesman extended to Europe, where the French considered Franklin a Renaissance man. The British, after Franklin endorsed revolution against the crown, considered him a dangerous traitor with a price on his head.

Of course, Franklin had his own media empire, and he was a postmaster, politician, firefighter, musician, and expert swimmer, among many things.

Here's a look at Franklin's top innovations, most of which are in use today somewhere in the United States.

Invention: The Franklin stove (1742). Previously, fireplaces in Colonial homes were inefficient and smoky. Franklin's stove gave homeowners a second option. The Franklin Stove, enclosed in iron, provided more heat with much less smoke, using much less wood. Franklin passed on patenting his invention because he thought it was for the greater good.

Invention: The lightning rod (circa 1753). Franklin used his understanding of electricity to develop a cheap solution to keep houses from burning down. The rod diverted electricity from a lightning strike into the ground near a building. They became very popular, and even King George III had one installed at his palace. The lightning rod has since undergone improvements, including a version from Nikola Tesla.

Invention or innovation: Bifocals (date unconfirmed). Historically, Franklin has been credited with inventing bifocals late in his life, as he needed corrective lenses to solve two vision problems. In recent years, there has been a debate about if Franklin was the first to invent bifocals, or if he was an early adopter that made them famous. An analysis from the College of Optometrists details the debate and suggests the technology existed in England in the 1760s, when Franklin was living there. Others believe Franklin invented the devices. Either way, he was the biggest "celebrity" in his day to use them.

Invention or innovation: The flexible catheter (1752). When Franklin's brother has having problems urinating due to kidney stones, the inventor came up with a practical, less painful solution than the rigid tube that doctors used for patients. The flexible catheter is still used today. There were apparently similar devices in Europe, but Franklin's was popular in America.

Invention: Key words to describe electricity. Franklin was famous for his experiments with electricity, which also endeared him with the scientific community in France (which helped his later diplomatic career). The late Professor Leo LeMay from the University of Delaware, who was an expert in all things Franklin, credited Franklin with adopting four words we all know today when it comes to electricity: battery, positive, negative, and charge. The words existed before Franklin's time but had different usage and meanings.

Bonus factoids: Things Franklin didn't invent. In 1997, LeMay posted a list of things Franklin didn't invent on the University of Delaware's website. These things included the first street light, the odometer, daylight savings time, the first volunteer fire company, and the first fire insurance company.

FRANKLIN AND ELECTRICITY- DID HE INVENT THE ELECTRICITY

Electricity was on people's minds in the 1740s, but not in the way we think about it today. People used electricity for magic tricks by creating sparks and shocks. Scientists conducted experiments with electricity, but scientific thinking about electricity had not changed much in hundreds of years. Electricity wasn't "useful" yet.

Benjamin Franklin was interested in electricity. Being a curious and inventive thinker, Franklin wanted to know more than just the popular tricks. He kept thinking about electricity and came up with a very important idea.

His idea was about electricity and lightning. Franklin noticed several similarities between the two: They both created light, made loud crashes when they exploded, were attracted to metal, had a particular smell, and more. Based on these observations, Franklin thought electricity and lightning were the same thing. A few people shared his belief, but no one had ever tested it.

Franklin wrote up his thoughts on electricity in several letters to a fellow scientist who lived in London. This scientist and other scientists in London thought Franklin's letters contained valuable information, so in 1751 they published them in a little book, Experiments, and Observations on Electricity.

One of the letters contained Franklin's plan for how to prove that electricity and lightning were the same. His plan required something tall, like a hill or a tall building, but Philadelphia had neither at the time. While Franklin was waiting for a tall building to be built, he came up with another plan. This one involved a key and a kite.

Franklin needed something to get close enough to the clouds to attract the lightning. He could not get up there since Philadelphia didn't have any hills or tall buildings. He did have a silk handkerchief, a couple of sticks and some string, so instead of getting himself up near the lightning, he flew a kite up to it. And it worked! Franklin and few other scientists in Europe (who did their own experiments) proved that lightning and electricity were the same thing.

But that wasn't enough for Franklin. He believed that this knowledge should be used for practical purposes.

What could be practical about lightning? Many folks knew what wasn't practical: having your house burn down because it was struck by lightning. Franklin thought he could help. He knew that lightning usually hit the highest part of a building. He also knew that the electrical current in lightning could start a fire. So he invented the lightning rod. A lightning rod is made of metal and is attached to the highest point on a house. The lightning hits the rod instead of the house, and the electrical current from the lightning goes into the ground and leaves the house undamaged. Franklin thought the lightning rod was his most important invention.

"No other town burying its great man, ever buried more of itself than Philadelphia with Franklin," wrote Carl Van Doren in his biography of Franklin.

Franklin himself had composed the black-bordered Pennsylvania Gazette which announced his death. Dr. Jones, Franklin's physician, informed the readers of Franklin's final illness. He had been suffering from empyema, pus filling in his lung brought on by attacks of pleurisy many years earlier. His temperature was high. This made breathing laborious, and he almost suffocated. After several days of breathing woes, the pain went away for a day, upon which he left his bed and asked that it be made properly so that he might have a dignified death. His daughter, Sally, told him that she hoped he would live many years more. "I hope not," he replied.

An abscess in Franklin's lung burst and he passed into a coma. He died on April 17, 1790, with his grandsons William Temple and Bennie at his side. Benjamin Franklin was 84 years old.

Franklin's graveOn April 21, the funeral procession gathered at the State House. Leading the cortege was the clergy of Philadelphia. Though Franklin was not a regular churchgoer by any means, he had aided the churches by raising funds to help their construction. His coffin was carried by the citizenry of Philadelphia. Dignitaries surrounded the Pall including Revolutionary Era Philadelphia mayor Samuel Powell, astronomer David Rittenhouse, and several members of Pennsylvania's Supreme Executive Council. Judges and current Philadelphia politicians were also in the mix.

They were followed by the printers of the city and their apprentices. Franklin always considered himself a leather apron man, a mechanic, a printer. "Keep they Trade, and thy Trade will keep Thee."

Then came members of the American Philosophical Society, which was co-founded by Franklin in the 1740's. Next came members of the College of Physicians. Franklin was a founding member of the Academy, which became the College of Philadelphia, which had created the College of Physicians, the first medical school in the country. The Society of Cincinnati found its way into the procession, though Franklin had derided their philosophy of making honor hereditary.

Franklin's graveOn the cortege wound, composed of citizens of all stripes, headed toward the Christ Church burial ground. It is estimated that 20,000 mourners gathered for the funeral. Bells of the city church's were muffled and tolled. When Franklin had arrived in Philadelphia's port on October 6, 1723, he was a broke runaway. Now the ships in the very same harbor Franklin had arrived in flew their flags at half-mast for the man who had enriched the world.

Franklin was buried beside his wife Deborah, who had preceded him in death by 25 years. His beloved son Francis Folger, who had died at age 4 from smallpox, was also in the family plot.

As a young man in 1728, Franklin had composed his own mock epitaph which read:

The Body of
B. Franklin
Printer;
Like the Cover of an old Book,
Its Contents torn out,
And stript of its Lettering and Gilding,
Lies here, Food for Worms.

But the Work shall not be really lost:

For it will, as he believ'd, appear once more,

In a new & more perfect Edition,

Corrected and Amended

By the Author.

He was born on January 6, 1706.

James Madison moved that the House of Representatives, then sitting in New York, wear mourning for a month.

France mourned.

In June, Count Mirabeau suggested that the French National Assembly should wear mourning as well. His suggestion also provides a fitting eulogy.

Would it not become us, gentlemen, to join in this religious act, to bear a part in this homage, rendered, in the face of the world, both to the rights of man and to the philosopher who has most contributed to extend their sway over the whole earth? Antiquity would have raised altars to this mighty genius, who, to the advantage of mankind, compassing in his mind the heavens and the earth, was able to restrain alike thunderbolts and tyrants. Europe, enlightened and free, owes at least a token of remembrance and regret to one of the greatest men who have ever been engaged in the service of philosophy and liberty. I propose that it be decreed that the National Assembly, during three days shall wear mourning for Benjamin Franklin.

Today thousands of tourists annually still come to pay their respect to Benjamin Franklin. His grave is visible through an iron gate at the southeast corner of 5th and Arch Streets. Pennies dot his tombstone, as local tradition claims that such a practice will bring the penny-tosser luck.

One must wonder what the author of Poor Richard's Almanack might think of such a practice though. On the one hand, a man famous for the line, "A penny saved, is a penny earned," would not like throwing money away; on the other hand surely Franklin would recognize, it is only "common cents" that we would look to him for inspiration.

1. He only had two years of formal education.

The man considered the most brilliant American of his age rarely saw the inside a classroom. Franklin spent just two years attending Boston Latin School and a private academy before joining the family candle and soap making business. By age 12, he was serving as an indentured apprentice at a printing shop owned by his brother, James. Young Benjamin made up for his lack of schooling by spending what little money he earned on books, often going without food to afford new volumes. He also honed his composition skills by reading essays and articles and then rewriting them from memory. Despite being almost entirely self-taught, Franklin later helped found the school that became the University of Pennsylvania and received honorary degrees from Harvard, Yale, the College of William and Mary, the University of St. Andrews and Oxford.

2. Franklin became a hit writer as a teenager.

After his brother James founded a weekly newspaper called the New England Courant in the 1720s, a 16-year-old Franklin began secretly submitting essays and commentary as "Silence Dogood," a fictitious widow who offered homespun musings on everything from fashion and marriage to women's rights and religion. The letters were hugely popular, and Mrs. Dogood soon received several marriage proposals from eligible bachelor's in Boston. Franklin penned 14 Dogood essays before unmasking himself as their author, much to his jealous brother's chagrin. Sick of the toil and beatings he endured as James' apprentice, the teenaged sensation then fled Boston the following year and settled in Philadelphia, the city that would remain his adopted hometown for the rest of his life.

3. He spent half his life in unofficial retirement.

Franklin arrived in Philadelphia in 1723 practically penniless, but over the next two decades he became enormously wealthy as a print shop owner, land speculator and publisher of the popular "Poor Richard's Almanack." By 1748, the 42-year-old was rich enough to hang up his printer's apron and become a "gentleman of leisure." Franklin's retirement allowed him to spend his remaining 42 years studying science and devising inventions such as the lightning rod, bifocal glasses and a more efficient heating stove. It also gave him the freedom to devote himself to public service. Despite never running for elected office, he served as a delegate to the Continental Congress and the Constitutional Convention, diplomat and ambassador to France and Sweden, the first postmaster general and the president of the Supreme Executive Council of Pennsylvania.

Armonica invented by Benjamin Franklin. (Credit: Andreas Feininger/The LIFE Picture Collection/Getty Images)

Armonica invented by Benjamin Franklin. (Credit: Andreas Feininger/The LIFE Picture Collection/Getty Images)

4. Franklin designed a musical instrument used by Mozart and Beethoven.

Among Franklin's more unusual inventions is his "glass armonica," an instrument designed to replicate the otherworldly sound that a wet finger makes when rubbed along the rim of a glass. He made his first prototype in 1761 by having a London glassmaker build him 37 glass orbs of different sizes and pitches, which he then mounted on a spindle controlled by a foot pedal. To play the instrument, the user would simply wet their fingers, rotate the apparatus and then touch the glass pieces to create individual tones or melodies. The armonica would go on to amass a considerable following during the 18th and early 19th centuries. Thousands were manufactured, and the likes of Mozart, Beethoven and Strauss all composed music for it. Franklin would later write that, "Of all my inventions, the glass armonica has given me the greatest personal satisfaction."

5. He was a reluctant revolutionary.

Franklin was among the last of the founding fathers to come out in favor of full separation from Britain. Having lived in London for several years and held royal appointments, he instead pushed for peaceful compromise and the preservation of the empire, once writing that, "every encroachment on rights is not worth a rebellion." When the Boston Tea Party took place in 1773, he dubbed it an "act of violent injustice on our part" and insisted that the East India Company should be compensated for its losses. Franklin had soured on the monarchy by the time he returned to the United States for the Second Continental Congress in 1775, but his past support for King George III earned him the suspicion of many of his fellow patriots. Before he publicly announced his support for American independence, few even suspected he might be a British spy.

6. Franklin created a phonetic alphabet.

While living in London in 1768, Franklin embarked on a project "to give the alphabet a more natural order." Annoyed by the many inconsistencies in English spelling, he devised his own phonetic system that ditched the redundant consonants C, J, Q, W, X, and Y and added six new letters, each designed to represent its own specific vocal sound. Franklin unveiled his "Scheme for a new Alphabet and a Reformed Mode of Spelling" in an essay published in 1779, but later scrapped the project after it failed to arouse public interest.

7. His son was a British loyalist.

Along with the two children he had with his wife, Deborah Read, Franklin also fathered an illegitimate son named William around 1730. The two were once close friends and partners—William helped Franklin with his famous kite experiment—but they later had a major falling out over the American

Revolution. While Franklin joined in calling for independence from the mother country, William remained a staunch Tory who branded the patriots "intemperate zealots" and refused to resign his post as the royal governor of New Jersey. He spent two years in a colonial prison for opposing the revolution and later became a leader in a loyalist group before moving to England at the end of the war. The elder Franklin never forgave his son for "taking up arms against me." He all but cut William out of his will, arguing, "the part he acted against me in the late war…will account for my leaving him no more of an estate he endeavored to deprive me of."

8. Franklin was a fashion icon in France.

In 1776, the Continental Congress sent Franklin to France to seek military aid for the revolution. The 70-year-old was already world renowned for his lighting experiments—the French even called their electrical experimenters "Franklinites"—but his fame soared to new heights after his arrival in Paris. Franklin capitalized on the French conception of Americans as rustic frontiersmen by dressing plainly and wearing a fur hat, which soon became his trademark and appeared in countless French portraits and medallions. Women even took to imitating the cap with oversized wigs in a style called "coiffure a la Franklin." When Franklin later traded the fur cap for a white hat during the signing of the 1778 treaty between the France and the United States, white colored headgear instantly became a fashion trend among the men of Paris.

9. He spent his later years as an abolitionist.

Franklin owned two slaves during his life, both of whom worked as household servants, but in his old age, he came to view slavery as a vile institution that ran counter to the principles of the American Revolution. He took over as president of a Pennsylvania abolitionist society in 1787, and in 1790 he presented a petition to Congress urging it to grant liberty "to those unhappy men who alone in this land of freedom are degraded into perpetual bondage." While the petition was ignored, Franklin kept up the fight until his death few months later, and even included a provision in his will that re□uired his daughter and son-in-law to free their slave to get their inheritance.

10. Franklin left Boston and Philadelphia an unusual gift in his will.

When he died in April 1790, Franklin willed 2,000 pounds sterling to his birthplace of Boston and his adopted home of Philadelphia. The largesse came with an unusual caveat: for its first 100 years, the money was to be placed in a trust and only used to provide loans to local tradesmen. A portion could then be spent, but the rest would remain off limits for another 100 years, at which point the cities could use it as they saw fit. Boston and Philadelphia followed Franklin's wishes, and by 1990 their funds were worth $4.5 million and $2 million, respectively. The two towns have since used the windfall to help finance the Franklin Institute in Philadelphia and the Benjamin Franklin Institute of Technology in Boston. Philadelphia also put some of its funds toward scholarships for students attending trade schools.

11. He's a member of the International Swimming Hall of Fame.

Franklin had a lifelong love of swimming that began during his childhood in Boston. One of his first inventions was a pair of wooden hand paddles that he used to propel himself through the Charles River, and he wrote of once using a kite to skim across a pond. While living in England in the 1720s, he displayed such an impressive array of swimming strokes during a dip in Thames that a friend offered to help him open his own swimming school. Franklin declined the offer, but he remained a proponent of swimming instruction for the rest of his life, once writing, "every parent would be glad to have their children skilled in swimming." His a□uatic exploits have since earned him an honorary induction into the International Swimming Hall of Fame.

Time is money.

BENJAMIN FRANKLIN, Advice to Young Tradesmen

In this world nothing can be said to be certain, except death and taxes.

BENJAMIN FRANKLIN, Letter to Jean Baptiste Le Roy, 13 Nov. 1789

Early to bed, and early to rise,
Makes a man healthy, wealthy, and wise.
BENJAMIN FRANKLIN, Poor Richard's Almanac, 1735

Success has ruined many a man.

BENJAMIN FRANKLIN, Poor Richard's Almanack, 1752

Necessity never made a good bargain.

BENJAMIN FRANKLIN, Poor Richard's Almanack, 1735

Marry'd in haste, we oft repent at leisure.

BENJAMIN FRANKLIN, Poor Richard's Almanac

Laziness travels so slowly that poverty soon overtakes him.

BENJAMIN FRANKLIN, The Way to Wealth

God helps them that helps themselves.

BENJAMIN FRANKLIN, Poor Richard's Almanac

Without Freedom of Thought, there can be no such thing as Wisdom; and no such thing as public Liberty, without Freedom of Speech.

BENJAMIN FRANKLIN, The New England Courant, Jul. 9, 1722

Three may keep a secret if two of them are dead.

BENJAMIN FRANKLIN, Poor Richard's Almanac, July 1735

Trust thy self, and another shall not betray thee.

BENJAMIN FRANKLIN, Poor Richard's Almanack, 1739

Dost thou love life? Then do not squander time, for that's the stuff life is made of.

BENJAMIN FRANKLIN, Poor Richard's Almanac

To lengthen thy life lessen thy meals.

BENJAMIN FRANKLIN, Poor Richard's Almanac

God heals and the doctor takes the fees.

BENJAMIN FRANKLIN, Poor Richard's Almanack, 1736

If you would know the value of money, go and try to borrow some; for he that goes a borrowing goes a sorrowing.

BENJAMIN FRANKLIN, Poor Richard's Almanac

No nation was ever ruined by trade.

BENJAMIN FRANKLIN, Thoughts on Commercial Subjects

Whatever begins in anger ends in shame.

BENJAMIN FRANKLIN, Poor Richard's Almanack, 1734

Three may keep a secret if two of them are dead.

He that lives upon hope will die fasting.

BENJAMIN FRANKLIN, Poor Richard's Almanac, preface, 1758

A countryman between 2 Lawyers, is like a fish between two cats.

BENJAMIN FRANKLIN, Poor Richard's Almanack, 1737

Little strokes fell great oaks.

BENJAMIN FRANKLIN, Poor Richard's Almanac, Aug. 1750

Experience keeps a dear school, yet fools will learn in no other.

BENJAMIN FRANKLIN, Poor Richard's Almanack, 1743

There never was a good war, or a bad peace.

BENJAMIN FRANKLIN, letter to Quincey, Sep. 11, 1783

Saying and Doing, have □uarrel'd and parted.

BENJAMIN FRANKLIN, Poor Richard's Almanack, 1756

The Game of Chess is not merely an idle amusement; several very valuable □ualities of the mind, useful in the course of human life, are to be ac□uired and strengthened by it, so as to become habits ready on all occasions; for life is a kind of Chess, in which we have often points to gain, and competitors or adversaries to contend with, and in which there is a vast variety of good and ill events, that are, in some degree, the effect of prudence, or the want of it. By playing at Chess then, we may learn: 1st, Foresight, which looks a little into futurity, and considers the conse□uences that may attend an action ... 2nd, Circumspection, which surveys the whole Chess-board, or scene of action: - the relation of the several Pieces, and their situations; ... 3rd, Caution, not to make our moves too hastily.

BENJAMIN FRANKLIN, "The Morals of Chess"

Democracy is two wolves and a lamb voting on what to have for lunch. Liberty is a well-armed lamb contesting the vote!

BENJAMIN FRANKLIN

Reading makes a full Man, Meditation a profound Man, Discourse a clear Man.

BENJAMIN FRANKLIN, Poor Richard's Almanack, 1738

Pride that dines on vanity, sups on contempt.

BENJAMIN FRANKLIN, "The Way to Wealth," The Life and Essays of Dr. Benjamin Franklin

Hide not your talents, they for use were made,
What's a sundial in the shade?
BENJAMIN FRANKLIN, Poor Richard's Almanac

Keep the eyes wide open before marriage and half shut afterwards.

BENJAMIN FRANKLIN, attributed, Wise Words and Quotes

Laws like to Cobwebs catch small Flies,
Great ones break thro' before your eyes.
BENJAMIN FRANKLIN, Poor Richard's Almanack, 1734

Wink at small faults; remember thou hast great ones.

BENJAMIN FRANKLIN, Poor Richard's Almanack, 1738

There are no fools so troublesome as those that have wit.

BENJAMIN FRANKLIN, Poor Richard's Almanack, 1741

In this world, nothing can be said to be certain, except death and taxes.

In 200 years will people remember us as traitors or heros? That is the ⬚uestion we must ask.

BENJAMIN FRANKLIN, letter to Thomas Jefferson, Mar. 16, 1775

I wish the Bald Eagle had not been chosen as the representative of our country; he is a bird of bad moral character; like those among men who live by sharping and robbing, he is generally poor and often very lousy. The turkey is a much more respectable bird.

BENJAMIN FRANKLIN, letter to Sarah Bache, Jan. 26, 1784

Beware of meat twice boiled, and an old foe reconciled.

BENJAMIN FRANKLIN, Poor Richard's Almanack, 1733

The most exquisite Folly is made of Wisdom spun too fine.

BENJAMIN FRANKLIN, Poor Richard's Almanack, 1746

He that falls in love with himself, will have no Rivals.

BENJAMIN FRANKLIN, Poor Richard's Almanack, 1739

Great Estates may venture more,

But little Boats should keep near Shore.

BENJAMIN FRANKLIN, Poor Richard's Almanack, 1758

If you would not be forgotten

As soon as you are dead and rotten,

Either write things worth reading,

Or do things worth the writing.

BENJAMIN FRANKLIN, Poor Richard's Almanack, 1738

Better slip with foot than tongue.

BENJAMIN FRANKLIN, Poor Richard's Almanack, 1734

The Doors of Wisdom are never shut.

BENJAMIN FRANKLIN, Poor Richard's Almanack, 1755

This is a short Benjamin Franklin biography that will show why he is one of the most famous inventors this world has ever known, and much more.

The Benjamin Franklin history begins with the answer to the common question of, "When was Benjamin Franklin born?" January 17, 1706 is the day he was born in Boston, Massachusetts. He was the 10th son and one of 17 children in his family. Even though he was only able to attend one year of school, Benjamin loved to read and by the age of 12 he was working as an apprentice to his brother James, who was a printer. Ben Franklin would help his brother compose pamphlets and set type, and then sell the products on the streets.

The next step in the Benjamin Franklin biography is his escape to Philadelphia. In early America it was frowned upon and even illegal to run away, but Franklin did it anyway in hopes of finding a job as a printer in New York. When that didn't work, he looked in New Jersey and eventually found work as an apprentice printer in Philadelphia.

During the 1730's and 1740's, Benjamin Franklin helped to start projects to pave and light the streets of Philadelphia, and to keep them clean. Benjamin Franklin's invention of the Library Company in 1731 was one of his biggest accomplishments during this era. This library had members who pooled their money to buy books from England, and then shared them.

In the Benjamin Franklin history, you will see that the reason that he is one of the most famous inventors in American history is that he had an amazing ability to recognize a problem, and then find a solution. Ben had become aware that the sick people in Philadelphia were not receiving the best care, so in 1751 he organized a group and formed the Pennsylvania Hospital.

Fires were also a problem at the time, so Benjamin decided to solve that problem as well. In 1736 he organized Philadelphia's Union Fire Company to deal with the fire problem. The famous Benjamin Franklin quote, "A ounce of prevention is worth a pound of cure," was about preventing fires.

He also took note of the incredible financial loss that was incurred by victims of fire, so he helped found the Philadelphia Contribution for Insurance Against Loss by Fire in 1752. That company is still in business today.

By 1749 Franklin's business ventures were thriving and he turned his attention to science and experiments. He had long been interested and involved in science and had even invented a heat-efficient stove, called the Franklin stove, in 1743. Now he finally had some time to devote to science, and he took full advantage of it. During the early part of the 1750's Franklin studied electricity. Ben achieved international fame with his kite experiment, which proved the nature of electricity and lightning.

During that time in the Benjamin Franklin biography, he began to take a more active role in politics. He traveled to England to represent Pennsylvania against the Penn family over who should represent the colony to England in 1757, and he stayed there until 1775. During that time, he worked as a representative for Pennsylvania, Georgia, New Jersey, and Massachusetts.

A very important part of the Benjamin Franklin biography is his return to America and his work towards Independence. Franklin was elected to the second Continental Congress and worked on the committee of five men to draft The Declaration of Independence.

While Thomas Jefferson did much of the writing, much of the contribution is Benjamin Franklin's.

In 1776, he signed the Declaration of Independence and then sailed to France to try and persuade them to help America in their fight for freedom. He was successful, and because of that, the United States is a free country today.

Benjamin Franklin was so loved and respected for all his accomplishments, that when he died on April 17, 1790 there were 20,000 people who attended his funeral! He truly was an amazing man.

THE BENJAMIN FRANKLIN EFFECT

Benjamin Franklin is known for many things...

Printer (built numerous printing businesses and was even responsible for printing all paper money for Pennsylvania & Delaware)

Newspaper Owner

Inventor (invented first original American musical instrument - the glass harmonica (Armonica), which even Bach & Beethoven wrote music for)

Musician (played violin, harp, guitar &, of course, the Armonica)

Inventor (Franklin stove, bifocal glasses, Lightening rod, Rocking chair, Odometer...)

Politician (one of the famous signatures on the Declaration of Independence)

Educator (formed an Academy for higher learning which, in 1791, was officially renamed... The University of Pennsylvania)

Developer (established the first circulation library for the colonies, first volunteer fire company, first insurance company, first hospital...)

Truly a gifted and insightful man, despite having been born the son of a soap and candlestick maker, with little or no education. Like many with drive and intelligence, he did not allow his lowly station to preclude him from learning all he could. He was passionate about self-improvement and went out of his way to network with anyone that had something he could learn. As a result, he became very adroit at human relations, at influencing and persuading others.

Perhaps one of the best-known persuasive techniques employed by Franklin, which is now credited to him and known as the Franklin Effect, plays against our intuitive belief that we do nice things for those we like and do not go out of our way to do anything nice for those we dislike.

What Franklin's study of human nature determined though is that our brain cannot uphold contradictory information. If we believe that we would only do nice things for those we like, then the logical implication is that if we do nice things for people... we must like them!

In his biography, Franklin described a particular situation and gentleman that was not a fan of his. In fact, this particular gentleman delivered a long speech to the legislature denigrating Franklin, in an effort to prevent his reelection into his role as Clerk of the General Assembly. Although Franklin won the role, he recognized that this colleague could gain more influence in the legislature that may impact Franklin's future opportunities. Franklin therefore realized he would need to turn this individual into a fan.

When faced with a similar dilemma, most of us would follow the more common route of going out of our way to say and do 'nice' things for and about the other party. However, Franklin was not willing to be seen as servile in any way, nor did he want his influence attempts to be obvious. Instead, he employed a much more subtle techni☐ue.

Franklin was well-known as an avid book collector, reader and library founder, all of which gave him a reputation as a man of exemplary tastes. His adversary also happened to have a private collection of books. Franklin, therefore,sent his adversary a letter asking if he could borrow a particular book from his private library. This book though, was very rare and difficult to come by. The rival, flattered by Franklin's re□uest, sent the book right away. Franklin read it and sent it back a week later, accompanied by a simple thank you. That's it!

The next time that the legislature met though, Franklin was approached by his adversary who engaged him in conversation for the first time. In Franklin's own words he explained that this gentleman "ever after manifested a readiness to serve me on all occasions, so that we became great friends, and our friendship continued to his death."

Most of us, in trying to build a bridge between ourselves and someone we dislike would think that the easiest way to do so would be to do a favor for them, to do something nice. Not so. They may feel the necessity to reciprocate in kind, but then they are merely paying off a debt and may even be angry that they 'owe' you. To shift their thinking about you permanently, you need a different approach. Instead of doing them a favour, you need to get them to do one for you. In so doing, their brains begin to modify their beliefs about you.

We believe that we would only do a favor for someone we like. Therefore, it follows that if we have done a favour for someone, then we must like them. We can't hold inconsistencies to be true in our brains, therefore our brains sort them to make sense of them. Getting someone to do you a favour will go alot further to making them feel more positively disposed toward you than your doing them a favour ever will.

So... stop spending all of your time doing for others and get them doing something for you! You'll seem a lot nicer for it!

Oh... and... could I ask you to do me a favour?

Please do not forget to give me a good review on amazon and follow my author and buy another book from me if you will not like it you can get your money back.

18311916R00032

Printed in Poland
by Amazon Fulfillment
Poland Sp. z o.o., Wrocław